ANCIENT SPIRITUAL DISCIPLINES

PRAYING
with the Saints

Jon M. Sweeney

PARACLETE PRESS
BREWSTER, MASSACHUSETTS

Praying with the Saints

2012 First Printing

ISBN 978-1-61261-249-2

Scripture quotations are taken from the *New Revised Standard Version*
Bible, copyright © 1989, Division of Christian Education of the
National Council of the Churches of Christ in the United States of
America. Used by permission. All rights reserved.

The Library of Congress has catalogued the original book *The Lure
of Saints*, from which the book is excerpted, under catalog number
2005003977.

10 9 8 7 6 5 4 3 2 1

Published by Paraclete Press
Brewster, Massachusetts
www.paracletepress.com

Printed in the United States of America

CONTENTS

INTRODUCTION

Saint Paul seemed to imply that every follower of Christ is a saint. He began his Second Letter to the Corinthians with this salutation: "Paul, an apostle of Christ Jesus by the will of God, and Timothy our brother, To the church of God that is in Corinth, including all the saints throughout Achaia: grace to you and peace from God our Father and the Lord Jesus Christ" (2 Corinthians 1:1–2). But when we talk about *the saints* we usually mean something more specific. We mean the exemplary figures, the important models of sanctity, who have defined over the centuries what it means to be Christian, and who are in heaven praying for us and rooting us on as we are on our own journeys to God.

Saints were once more familiar to Christians than they are today. The simple expression on the face of a popular saint in a piece of art or on a statue in church could mean a great deal because people were familiar with the stories of the saints. The uneducated of the Middle Ages—as well as nearly every catechumen raised in the days of the *Penny Catechism*—would have quickly known St. Bernard of Montjoux by the dog at his side, St. Francis of Assisi pictured with a wolf, a bleeding wound upon the body of St. Roch, a monstrance in the hands of St. Clare, St. Augustine with a pen or book in his hands, bees around St. Isidore of Seville, and St. Patrick stepping on snakes. But most of us don't grow up in the church today as our parents and grandparents once did.

Even when we don't know these stories the way people once did, they still have power. The combination of sin and victory over sin in their lives highlights other universal human experiences such as desire, shame, loss, darkness, light, and love. The life of Blessed Angela of Foligno exemplifies all of these themes at once, as does that of the more recent St. Padre Pio. (See below for why some saints are called "Blessed," while others are "Saint," abbreviated "St.")

Some saints are more human than others. St. Jerome, for example, was often downright grumpy in many of his relationships. His saintliness did not come about due to pleasantness. And the perhaps soon-to-be-saint, Dorothy Day, cofounder of the Catholic Worker movement, was a single mother, had an abortion long before it was legal to do so, and lived in Hollywood for a time working as a screenwriter. After her conversion she became convinced of the need to dedicate her life to helping the poor and disadvantaged, the homeless and hungry, and to working toward peace. It was Day who once famously explained she never wanted to be made a saint. Why? "You cannot dismiss me that easily!" she declared. She was afraid that, once a person becomes a saint, he or she becomes more like the statue in the garden than a real person. Hers is a good reminder to us to make sure that the lives of the saints remain relevant in our lives.

Long before I became a Catholic, I was raised in a kind of fundamentalist Protestantism that dispensed with all symbols; nevertheless, I found myself drawn to the paintings of saints. I was both fascinated and revolted by them. And the more gruesome the better: blood flowing from Christ's open wounds on the cross, Salome's satisfied expression as St. John the Baptist's head was separated from his body at her whim. I sat for hours and gawked. This was the Bible in an entirely new light, nothing like the more rational religion of my childhood. I was drawn to the saints, but I didn't know why. I felt the lure of their images and the stories of their lives, and the strangeness of it all seemed, somehow, terribly relevant to my life.

Their stories are sometimes easy to distill down into one or two important symbols or details. St. Francis of Assisi, for example, appears in art (or on the old saint cards) embarrassed over his delicately bleeding hands, feet, and side—as the bearer of the first stigmata, afflicted with the five wounds of Christ. The aforementioned St. Jerome, a scholar and a solitary, sits with his equally great lion attendant; it was Jerome who pulled a thorn from a lion's paw, giving birth to tales penned by storytellers from the Brothers Grimm to Walt Disney. The beautiful St. Lucia carries her lovely eyes, recently gouged out by her own hand, in a goblet so she can give them to the suitor whom she spurned and who then gave her up to martyrdom for being a Christian. And St. Lawrence, with an equal measure of nonchalance for his own fate, stands blithely beside the griddle that cooked him to a crisp.

In the years since my gory and eye-opening introduction to the Church's heroes, I have spent thousands of hours reading about saints, talking and writing about them, making my own prayers to saints, and searching the Bible and Christian tradition for what it means to be a saint—in the past and today. I have written and edited several books about St. Francis of Assisi, the saint to whom I feel the greatest connection. And I have learned that saints are for everybody.

I invite you to join me as we explore the world of saints and discover a variety of ways in which the saints are already a part of our lives. In the chapters that follow, you will find many profiles of ancient, medieval, and modern figures representing both East and West, the sublime and the unusual. You will be encouraged to find the saint who "speaks" most directly to you—and you will discover a variety of ways to pray with their help.

ONE

Who Are They? How Did It All Begin?

ANGELS

The first saints were angels with wings, according to the chronology of the Bible. First among them was St. Michael the archangel, one of the most common saints depicted in art.

Before the six days of creation, when God resided in heaven with the heavenly host, there was a very important and exalted angel by the name of Lucifer. He was so beautiful that he was known as the "Son of Morning." One day, Lucifer revolted, recruiting many other angels who no longer wished to be ruled by God. According to legend, it was St. Michael who then rallied the good angels against Lucifer and the other rebellious ones, literally booting them out of heaven. The book of Revelation says that Michael will once again battle Lucifer, "holding in his hand the key to the bottomless pit and a great chain" with which to bind him for 1,000 years (Revelation 20:1).

Frequently shown in paintings armed to the teeth and battling a demon or devil, St. Michael became a patron saint in times of war. Combatants prayed for his intercession and attributed victories to him. Apparitions of Michael were reported in France in the sixth and seventh centuries, including at Mont-Saint-Michel, where a famous shrine to the angelic saint still stands. Many churches are dedicated to Michael and the other two archangels mentioned in Scripture: St. Gabriel, the messenger of the annunciation to Mary, and St. Raphael, the great helper of Tobit and also possibly the angel responsible for the healing power of "the stirring of the water" at the Bethesda pool in Jerusalem (John 5:2–9).

Early ivory carving of St. Michael with scepter and holding the orb of earth in his trusted hand.

Angels reappear throughout Christian history in the lives of the saints. Visitations from angels, who are sometimes disguised as strangers or animals or birds, often punctuate turning points and crises of vocation in saints' lives, and angels appear as well to deliver divine messages. Even fallen angels appear from time to time. Brendan, the seafaring Irish saint, speaks to a bird that has landed on the prow of his boat, asking it, "Who are you, and why are all of you here?" The bird responds that it is one of the fallen angels who made the mistake of following Lucifer, now left to wander the earth singing God's praises rather than doing the same at God's feet in heaven.

THE APOSTLES

The Apostles of Jesus Christ were among the first and most important saints after his death and resurrection. It is they who set out to tell the story of the life and ministry of Jesus around the world. Each of them (except for Judas, of course) is identified with intrepid courage and a journey to some part of the world carrying the Great Commission. Most of them died at the hands of those whom they had come to save, and each of them—Peter, Andrew, James the son of Zebeedee, John, Philip, Bartholomew, Thomas, Matthew, James the son of Alphaeus, Thaddaeus, Simon, and Matthias (who replaced Judas)—is a saint.

There are plenty of other saints from the stories of the New Testament Gospels, too. For example, St. Joseph was the faithful father of Jesus. St. Mary Magdalene was one of the most passionate followers of Christ and the one who first believed in his resurrection (see Luke 24). St. Dismas the Good Thief witnessed to the truth as he died beside Jesus on the cross (see page 27, below). And there are many, many others. Of course there's also the Blessed Virgin Mary, who is so special in the pantheon of Christian saints that we don't usually refer to her simply as St. Mary because she is in a category all by herself. (See chapter 3.)

EARLY MARTYRS AND HEROES

The early Christians understood certain passages of Scripture much more intimately than we do today. Imagine, for instance, how the citizens of any large city of the Roman Empire would have heard these words from Psalm 116 during the worst decades of persecution of Christians: "Precious in the sight of the LORD is the death of his faithful ones" (v. 15). The early Christian martyrs were witnesses to their convictions to the point of a horrible death.

According to the legends of the church, martyrs enjoy an immediate and special place in heaven as a reward for their final deeds; Islam did not originate this idea. When Michelangelo painted his awe-inspiring *Last Judgment* on the altar wall of the Sistine

Chapel in Rome (1533–41), he pictured Christ as a Judge presiding over a vast scene, with the Virgin Mary to his right and famous martyrs to his left. St. Peter holds his papal keys; St. Catherine, the wheel that tortured her; St. Sebastian, a handful of arrows plucked from his body; St. Bartholomew, his own peeled skin in one hand and the knife used to do it in the other. A few nameless saints hold the crosses on which they were crucified. Martyrs had a special place for eternity.

In the era of the martyrs it was easy to make a saint. A local bishop could name any martyr as someone to be remembered, imitated, and venerated. It was the decision of a local community, signified by a local bishop, to continue to "be in communion" (*communicarent*) with a man or a woman who had lived a holy life and died a noble death—confessing faith and dying at the hands of others.

Martyrs were sainted so soon after their deaths at this time because the believers who were left living expected to see them again imminently. The early church was waiting for the prompt return of Jesus, and a community of saints was understood to be waiting in their graves to be reunited with the living. In these early days, from approximately AD 90 to the middle of the third century—just after the Gospel of John and some of the later epistles were written but before they were all collected into what became the accepted canon of the New Testament—the first Christians lived in heightened

anticipation of the Second Coming, believing that
the world would soon end. During these early days,
the memory of the martyrs and their teachings
were treasured but rarely preserved in any lasting
way. Why bother to spend time and effort preserving memories of loved ones and friends when one
expected to see them again so soon, in heaven? It
would have seemed as foolish as buying lakefront
property when you know that the world will soon
be coming to an end. St. John seemed to know this
when he quoted Jesus as saying,

> Very truly, I tell you, the hour is coming, and
> is now here, when the dead will hear the voice
> of the Son of God, and those who hear will live.
> For just as the Father has life in himself, so he
> has granted the Son also to have life in himself;
> and he has given him authority to execute judg-
> ment, because he is the Son of Man. Do not be
> astonished at this; for the hour is coming when
> all who are in their graves will hear his voice
> and will come out—those who have done good,
> to the resurrection of life, and those who have
> done evil, to the resurrection of condemnation.
> (John 5:25–29)

St. Stephen was the first martyr. Jewish by
birth, he was one of the most important early
followers of the apostles after the death of Christ.
He was a deacon of the early church and was

stoned for preaching that Jews no longer needed the temple in Jerusalem or the Law of Moses; these were temporary and were replaced by the person of Jesus Christ, he said (Acts 6). The stones that killed him are kept, along with his bones, in Rome still today. Stephen was also very beautiful. Many painted images of Stephen have been thought to border on the erotic, as they combine his violent death with the beauty of his physical appearance.

St. Polycarp was perhaps the most important martyr in the early church. He died in 155 and was the last personal disciple of one of the original twelve apostles (St. John). Polycarp was the bishop of Smyrna, in today's Turkey. He was the most venerable leader of the early Christians against heresy and was known for his early attempts to reconcile Eastern and Western Christian practice (such as the dating and celebration of Easter). He was martyred in Smyrna during a period when Christians were accused of atheism for their refusal to worship the emperor. Polycarp movingly refused to deny his faith before a crowd of his captors, and each step in the process of his trial and death was recorded by his own disciples.

St. Polycarp was burned at the stake, but witnesses said that the fire could not consume him. This caused the executioner to stab him with a dagger. So much blood flowed from his side that the fire was quenched with it, and, his disciples' record reads, "out came a dove" from his pierced body, a symbol to Christians that the soul lives on and flees straight to heaven.

The veneration of St. Polycarp—for his extraordinary witness and ministry to the faithful both before and after his martyrdom—began immediately after his death. In the *Epistle of the Church of Smyrna*, we read of how Polycarp's martyrdom came to be celebrated on the anniversary of his death (February 23):

> Thus we at last gathered up his bones, which are more precious to us than precious gems and finer than gold, and laid them to rest where it was proper to do so. There the Lord will permit us to come together in gladness and joy to celebrate the birthday of his martyrdom.

Not all the martyrs lived during Roman times. One of the most famous martyrs in history is St. Thomas Becket, who was born in London in 1118. While still in his thirties, Thomas was named chancellor of England by King Henry II, a post that made him both a personal adviser to the throne and an ambassador to the Vatican. Several years later, the king expanded Thomas's responsibilities by naming him archbishop of Canterbury. Pope Alexander III confirmed the appointment (for this was four hundred years before the Church of England split from Rome).

St. Thomas was a person of devotion, prayer, and real virtue. He strove to execute his duties to

God and church with faithfulness, and eventually Thomas's independent spirit put him at odds with King Henry. After several disputes pitted the two men against each other, and Thomas fled England and then returned, the king announced, "Someone needs to rid me of my archbishop!" A group of knights, anxious for favors from the throne, rode to Canterbury and hunted Thomas down in the cathedral. He was a saint the moment his split head hit the cathedral floor. Pilgrims began visiting Canterbury Cathedral as soon as word spread of the murder. King Henry II himself traveled to Canterbury Cathedral less than four years after the murder that he had caused, doing penance for his sins. Martyrs have the power to effect great change through their deaths.

We also have Christian martyrs in our own time. Many of us might remember Oscar Romero, the archbishop of San Salvador, who was murdered on March 24, 1980, while celebrating Mass at the altar of a small hospital chapel. He was killed by a single gunshot to the chest by a soldier on the orders of a top El Salvadoran general. His cause for sainthood is ongoing.

Romero had united himself with the poor against the evils of El Salvador's military-ruled government, which had harassed and murdered hundreds of trade unionists, human-rights workers, priests, and others who spoke up against these atrocities. The United States, fearing the spread of communism in Latin America, supported the El Salvadoran government with arms and military advisers, even after Romero sent many pleas to then-president Jimmy Carter, and even after Romero's murder. More killings occurred after Romero's death as well, including those of four Maryknoll and Ursuline nuns nine months later and six Jesuit priests, their housekeeper, and his daughter in 1989.

Like many martyrs before him, Romero knew that his death would take on special meaning. Two weeks before it happened, Romero told an interviewer: "I do not believe in death without resurrection. If they kill me, I will be resurrected in the Salvadoran people." He is already a saint in the eyes of the people of El Salvador.

Since the earliest days, Christians have celebrated the death dates of saints rather than their birthdays. This innovation, definitely not something inherited from earlier Jewish or pagan traditions, is distinctive to Christianity. The reason is very simple: a martyr's death day becomes, in effect, his or her new birthday, in heaven—a far more important occasion for celebration. Also, the death day of a martyr was far easier to authenticate and remember than was his or her birthday.

It was during the rule of the Roman emperor Diocletian (284–305) that the first mention was made of the establishment of All Saints' Day, now November 1. During Diocletian's hideous rein, so many Christians were martyred that it became impossible to commemorate each on a specific day. All Saints' Day was established for the purpose of venerating them all.

HERMITS, MONKS, AND NUNS

After the era of the martyrs, whose blood is the foundation of the church, we enter the time of the desert fathers and mothers, monks, and other hermits—those unusual people who left behind the relative comfort of cities and families for a more severe experience of God. Following the example of some of the prophets in the Hebrew Scriptures, who lived alone for long lengths of time in the desert or the forest outside the city, Jesus also spent time alone in the wilderness and in the desert. St. John the Baptist, of course, did so as well. Hermits of the faith have always had one primary responsibility: to provide spiritual counsel, grounded in their prophetic distance from what is ordinary.

St. Mary of Egypt (ca. 344–ca. 421) was one of the most famous early women hermits. As a young woman she fled Alexandria, where she had been engaged in prostitution, and then lived in the deserts of Egypt, becoming the patron saint of penitents. Later, throughout the Middle Ages, anchorites and anchoresses often lived as hermits in small rooms (or cells) attached to the outside of parish churches. One small window allowed the hermit to participate in worship, and another window faced out so that he or she could receive guests who sought wisdom. Blessed Julian of Norwich was such an anchoress in England in the early fifteenth century.

The first desert-hermit saint was St. Paul the Hermit (d. 342). Paul had another reason besides seeking a deeper experience of God for fleeing the city—to avoid generic faith and universalized religious practice, which had already begun to creep into the Roman Empire in the decades following Constantine the Great's conversion to Christianity in 312. According to tradition, a raven brought Paul, who lived in a cave, a loaf of bread from time to time.

St. Antony of Egypt (d. 356), also known as St. Antony the Great, is recognized as the founder of monasticism. Like many saints before and after him, Antony was born into a wealthy and influential family but left that behind in order to pursue a deeper relationship with God. One legend has it that Antony made this decision one day after hearing Matthew 19:21 read during worship. When disciples began to gather around Antony, he was forced to abandon his solitary life and founded the first monastery, an interconnected set of hermit cells. We know a great deal about Antony because of the diligent work of another saint, Athanasius of Alexandria, his student, who wrote the first hagiography on Antony in the middle of the fourth century. It was widely published and read even in those days long before paper and printing presses, and it influenced thousands of men and women to become monks and solitaries in the late Roman Empire.

St. Benedict of Nursia (d. ca. 550) is recognized as one of the founders of monasticism in community. He, too, began his religious life as a hermit, but after spending several years alone in a cave in Italy (known today as the *Sacro Speco*, "the holy grotto"), Benedict decided to found a "school of service" to God, a place where he would help other men lead holy lives through the monastic vocation. Named the patron saint of Europe for his role in schooling that region of the world in Christianity, Benedict learned from the hermits and monks who had come before him (Sts. Pachomius, Augustine, Basil the Great, John Cassian) and who had also written Rules, or guides, for the monastic life. Benedict's Rule became the norm for all of Western monasticism. It emphasizes the role of an abbot in strengthening a community of monks, the praying of the Divine Office in community, and the welcoming of guests as if they were Christ himself. He wrote his influential Rule while living in community, and within a few years he had founded at least twelve monasteries, which functioned like religious colleges for young and old alike. The feast of St. Benedict is celebrated each year on July 11. (More on the feasts of saints can be found in chapter 4.)

St. Benedict, by Perugino (d. 1523), a painting in the Vatican Museums. The saint holds his quill and book, representing the influential Rule for monks that he authored.

Among the most important monastic saints, we also cannot forget the monks of early medieval Ireland. They were known for their studiousness, and if it wasn't for their extraordinary dedication to copying and preserving the manuscripts of early Christianity we wouldn't know much of what we now know about the first centuries of our faith.

By the twelfth and thirteenth centuries, we see the awakening of Europe and all of Christendom by the mendicant religious orders, reform movements within monasticism. This is when the Franciscans, Carmelites, Dominicans, Servites, and Augustinians were all born. They took vows of poverty and usually became friars, rather than monks, leaving behind the cloister. Most important of all the mendicants was the selfless ministry of the *Poverello* or "little poor man" from Assisi, St. Francis (d. 1226)—the world's most popular saint. He and his early spiritual brothers and sisters, the Franciscans and the Sisters of St. Clare, are the joyful fools of popular legend. Following the teachings of Jesus to the letter, they lived in voluntary poverty and they were both revered and ridiculed for their simple lives. Despite their reputation as lighthearted and full of joy, the Franciscans also became known as great mediators of conflicts (during the Crusades and now in the West Bank of Israel/Palestine) and excellent scholars (they founded many of the first universities of Europe).

Next we come to the remarkable saints produced by the Catholic Counter-Reformation in the sixteenth and early seventeenth centuries. St. John of the Cross (d. 1591) is, still today, an inspiration to many through his poetry and other writings on "the dark night of the soul," that darkness that is trusting faith and leads to deeper knowledge of God. And St. Ignatius of Loyola (d. 1556), author of the most influential book for Christian meditation ever written, the *Spiritual Exercises*, inspired Catholics to see the beauty and strength of their ancient tradition even after the reforms of Luther and others. He founded the Society of Jesus, the Jesuits, an order of religious men who desired to live an active (in the world) vocation, rather than a purely contemplative (in a cloister) one. Ignatius loved the stories of the early and medieval saints, although he occasionally disapproved of their asceticism and passiveness, and he taught their stories to thousands through his preaching. The Jesuits also focused their efforts on hearing confessions, urging personal conversion, and fighting heresy.

Now, it would be impossible to introduce you to all of the saints in one book. Libraries have been filled with the books that do that! So, here, is a brief tour from A–Z of some of the other most memorable—and, in some cases, lesser known, saints.

AN A TO Z OF THE FAMOUS AND THE NOT-SO-FAMOUS

An icon writer (they "write" icons rather than "paint" them) will tell you that it is the eyes of the figure that are the most important feature. These are the last things written on an icon—which is intended to be a presence of the person represented. If you connect with the eyes in an icon, if they seem perhaps to "speak" to you, that icon and that saint may be meaningful for your vocation and situation in life. Icons can convey a sense that the saints they represent are immediately present with you. Hopefully, you will connect with at least one of the following stories in the way that you might connect with an icon. These saints represent a wide cross-section of Christians throughout the ages and the world—men and women, ancient and modern, East and West, North and South, strange and typical.

St. Andrew Kim Tae-gon. Korean Catholics are rightly proud of the origins of the Catholic faith in Korea; it was built on the blood of martyrs, much as was the church of the West almost two millennia earlier. Andrew (d. 1846) was the first native Korean priest, having been ordained by French missionaries in Shanghai, China. Christianity was illegal in Korea at this time, and nearly one hundred people had been martyred there since the beginning of the nineteenth century. "The usual method of martyrdom was to be tied to a cross, taken on an oxcart to the place of execution, stripped naked, and then beheaded. Their heads and bodies would be publicly exposed for three days to terrify other Christians."[1] Within days of his ordination, Andrew returned to Korea as a leader of the underground movement. Soon, he was captured and thrown into prison, where he wrote a pastoral letter that sustained the fledgling church, much as St. Paul's letters, written while he was in prison, sustained the early church. Andrew was martyred, and 138 years later Pope John Paul II canonized him from the Seoul Cathedral.

St. Brendan. Known as the sailor-monk, or the seafaring saint, Brendan (d. ca. 575) spent most of his adult life in a boat with the men who followed him, sailing from island to island in the Irish Sea. He founded monastic communities wherever he went, which may have included Scotland, Wales, and parts of Britain as well. Brendan's navigations became legendary; like the stories of Beowulf, they were repeated for centuries. These charming tales liken the places of Brendan's sea travels, which were often islands with inhabitants either friendly and lovely or hostile and uninhabitable, to places of the Apocalypse (heaven, purgatory, hell). Other tales relate nonspiritual myths, such as the one in which Brendan and his fellow seafaring monks land on an island and, upon kindling a fire, realize that the island is not in fact solid land but rather an enormous sea monster.

St. Catherine of Siena. Known as a great thinker and debater, Catherine (d. 1380) is also one of the most intriguing figures in history. She converted pagan philosophers and argued with popes (Pope Urban VI's men once even tried to arrange for her murder, unsuccessfully). Always criticized by men for having strong opinions and presuming to teach, Catherine once retorted to a bishop that he was ordaining "boys and not men" to be priests. She was declared a doctor of the church in 1970, an honor long overdue.

St. Dismas the Good Thief. The last person Jesus spoke to before he died on the cross (Luke 23:39–43), Dismas was considered a saint by the early church on account of his clear faith in Jesus as the Son of God. (The Scriptures do not give us Dismas's name; however, tradition does that.) Jesus was a friend to sinners, and perhaps Dismas had heard Christ's teachings before that day on Golgotha, when Dismas said to him, "Jesus, remember me when you come into your kingdom." Jesus replied, "Today you will be with me in Paradise." The early church regarded the day of their death and new life as March 25.

St. Elizabeth Ann Seton. The first American-born person to be canonized, in 1975, Elizabeth was born two centuries earlier in New York City as the American colonies were heading to war with England. She was the child of devout Anglican parents, and she became known as "the Protestant sister of charity" as a young married woman, when she used her substantive resources to aid widows and children. But when her husband, William, suddenly went bankrupt and soon after died of tuberculosis, Elizabeth converted to Catholicism. It was 1805, and there were relatively few Catholics in the United States; she was almost thirty years old. A few years later, she founded the Daughters of Charity, a religious community for women, and became known as Mother Seton for her caring and able approach to both administrative duties and personal relationships. The order founded schools for needy children, charging tuition only to those who could afford it.

St. Frances Xavier Cabrini. Another American saint, Mother Frances (d.1917) became the patron saint of immigrants, as she devoted her life to caring for those who came to this country, largely from European countries, in the late nineteenth and early twentieth centuries. An immigrant herself, from Italy, she came to the United States in 1889. She was canonized immediately following the Second World War by Pope Pius XII.

St. Helena. Her life is a fascinating combination of fact and fiction; whether true or not, her story is one of the most important tales of the Roman era of the church. Helena's son, Constantine, became the first Christian emperor of the Roman Empire in 312 after earning a victory in battle that he felt God had given him. Helena converted to Christ with her son, as did much of the empire. Several years later, as part of her new devotion to God, Helena made a pilgrimage to the Holy Land. Having been told in a dream the whereabouts of the true cross of Christ, she led an excavation to unearth it. With the cooperation of Macarius, the bishop of Jerusalem and later a saint himself, and with the aid of the power represented by her son, Helena first destroyed the heathen temple to Venus that stood on Calvary at that time. Eventually, after much digging, the cross of Christ, as well as those of the two thieves, was found, and, according to legend, the nails and the inscription board that had been hung above our Lord were discovered as well.

The Vision of St. Helena, by Paolo Veronese (d. 1588). Two child angels show the saint the whereabouts of the true cross in a dream.

St. Ivo of Kermartin. There are very few civil lawyers on the calendar of saints! Ivo (d. 1303) was a lawyer in France at a time when corruption was taken for granted and impartiality was almost nonexistent. A model for how the law should function in any age, Ivo, who was trained as both a canon (religious) and a civil judge, advocated settlements out of court whenever possible. He practiced a strict, monastic-style spirituality in order to ensure that his motivations were as righteous as possible. He was known as a defender of the poor, or those who could not afford adequate legal representation, and as a pardoner who always sought to give people a second chance whenever possible. Toward the end of his life, Ivo also became a priest.

St. Jerome in the Desert, by Lord Frederic Leighton (d. 1896). The saint performs penance in the wilderness before a cross of his own making while his faithful lion faces the sunset.

St. Jerome. A symbol of both repentance and scholarship, Jerome was a serious student of the classics when he was converted to a desire to know the Scriptures instead. He was the first to translate the Bible into Latin (known as the Vulgate), and he is known to history as one of the four Latin doctors of the church (with Sts. Ambrose, Augustine, and Gregory the Great). He was cantankerous and ill-mannered toward those in authority, and he did not last long in Rome. When his friend Pope Damasus died, Jerome settled in Bethlehem and eventually founded a monastery there, near the birthplace of Jesus. Jerome died in about 420.

St. Katharine Drexel. Another American who has been beatified or canonized, this Philadelphian died in 1955. She was known as Mother Katharine throughout her religious life, which formally began at age thirty when she joined the Sisters of Mercy as a nun. The child of wealthy parents (her father was a banker who left her a fortune in the millions), Katharine gave her assets and herself completely to the poor. She was specifically drawn to the plight of Native Americans throughout the Western U.S. and African Americans in U.S. cities, who suffered poverty and a lack of educational resources. In 1891 she founded a new religious congregation (similar to an order) called Sisters of the Blessed Sacrament. The sisters built schools—more than one hundred of them. Mother Katharine and her sisters were an important part of the early civil rights movement in America and were often threatened by the Ku Klux Klan. One Catholic scholar recounts the following anecdote: "Her sisters walked the streets of New

Orleans and Harlem during the 1950s and were jeered at and called 'Nigger sisters.' When they described the name-calling to Mother Katharine, she simply asked, 'Did you pray for them?'"[2]

St. Louis-Marie Grignion de Montfort. Known for his extraordinary devotion to the Virgin Mary, Montfort authored the most important book in the history of Mariology, *True Devotion to Mary.* He was born in Brittany, France, in a small town named Montfort, from which he took his surname. He was ordained a priest in 1700, and his primary vocation was as a "missionary apostolic," or traveling preacher. Louis de Montfort founded two religious orders, both of which are active in the United States today: the Montfort Fathers and Brothers and the Daughters of Wisdom.

St. Mary Magdalene. Considered to be one of the true apostles of Christ, this St. Mary is one of the most fascinating saints in history. Interest in her life and her role in Jesus's life has been sparked in recent years by Dan Brown's best-selling novel *The Da Vinci Code.* Some legends identify her with the prostitute in Luke 7 and with the woman who perfumed the feet of Jesus in Luke 10 and John 12. Regardless, Mary Magdalene was the most important witness of the Resurrection according to the Gospel accounts. She was a disciple of Jesus and a friend and adviser of the first apostles.

Paintings of St. Mary Magdalene always show her physical beauty. Here she holds a lamp, an image of her waiting and looking for the resurrected Lord. St. Clare of Assisi is beside her in this painting by Luca Signorelli (d. 1523).

St. Nicholas of Flüe. The patron saint of Switzerland was a hermit, a layperson, and the father of ten children. These are remarkable facts taken together, and Nicholas was a remarkable and enigmatic figure. It seems that he was a local government leader, employed as a magistrate while still a young man. But while his children were still at home, his wife gave him permission to live much of the time in a small hermitage, practicing various forms of asceticism (he reportedly ate only the Eucharist for many years) and meditating on the Passion, as did many other members of the Friends of God, a lay movement once popular throughout Switzerland. During his stays in the hermitage, Nicholas became a popular spiritual director, even advising government officials to the point of helping the country avoid a civil war.

Flannery O'Connor, the twentieth-century American writer, may one day be deserving of saintly recognition. She was a devout Catholic, and her fiction (such as *A Good Man Is Hard to Find*) startles with its use of sometimes violent and always arresting images and characters who find grace and redemption in the unlikeliest of places.

Venerable Pierre Toussaint. Born into slavery on the French colony of Santo Domingo (modern-day Haiti), Pierre was "purchased" by Marie Elizabeth Berard and taken to New York City in 1787. Pierre worked as a hairdresser there and was soon in demand among New York's elite. Pierre was able to make and save some money, and he purchased his sister's freedom from their master, but not his own. Berard was recently widowed, and Pierre appears to have willingly chosen to remain a slave in order to care for her and allow her to avoid embarrassment. Finally granted his own freedom when Berard passed away, Pierre married Juliette Noel, whose freedom he had also purchased. He spent the rest of his years making money in order to give it away. Pierre was dedicated to aiding immigrants new to America; he housed orphans, schooled black children he discovered on the streets, and cared for plague victims, as Blessed Teresa later did in Calcutta. He died at about the age of ninety in 1853. His case for sainthood was officially opened in 1968, and in 1990 his body was exhumed and reburied under the main altar of St. Patrick's Cathedral in New York City.

Queen of Heaven. As we've already noted, the Blessed Virgin Mary is usually regarded as the most important of all the saints. There are many honorific titles for her and many feasts celebrated for her. One of these is Queen of Heaven. The Christians of the late Roman Empire most likely adopted the term from popular religion, as the goddess Isis (and others) also held this title. The title Queen of Heaven recognizes Mary's role as "blessed among women" (as uttered in the Hail Mary) and as queen, in that she was the mother to the child who assumed "the throne of his ancestor David" (Luke 1:32). It was not until the mid-twentieth century that the Catholic church made a special feast day for the Queen of Heaven, reminding Catholics of her leadership role over angels, patriarchs, prophets, apostles, martyrs, confessors, virgins, and all saints, as prayed for centuries in the Litany of the Blessed

Virgin, approved by Pope Xystus (or Sixtus) V in 1587. One of the most popular Catholic hymns is the *Salve Regina*, or "Hail, Holy Queen."

St. Rita of Cascia. One of the most popular uses of the word *saint* focuses on sweet forbearance in the midst of terrible trouble. We look at a child who smiles despite suffering and say, "(S)he is such a saint!" Well, Rita is one saint who gives rise to such pronouncements, since her life was so pathetically sad. She was married for eighteen years to an unfaithful and abusive husband. One night he was murdered, and soon afterward Rita's only two children, both sons, also died. Childless and widowed, she became a nun and devoted herself to prayer. It is said that Rita prayed and meditated so fervently on the Passion that she received wounds on her forehead like those of Christ from the crown of thorns. Rita eventually died of tuberculosis (in 1447), but immediately after her death she became renowned for intercessory miracles. She joins St. Jude as the other popular saint of desperate causes.

Seven. There are four **Sevens** among the saints. First are the **Seven Apostles of Bulgaria**, seven men who brought Christianity to the Slavs in the Middle Ages. Then there are the **Seven Brothers**. According to legend, these sons of St. Felicity were each martyred during one of the early Roman persecutions of Christians. As the story goes, Felicity witnessed each execution before her own life was taken. The **Seven Servite Founders** were devout men from wealthy homes in thirteenth-century Florence who formed a new religious order of friars after the example of St. Francis of Assisi, but they were devoted to honoring the Virgin Mary. They emphasized Mary's "seven sorrows" as well as her "seven joys." Finally, there are the **Seven Sleepers of Ephesus**. These men of Ephesus reputedly slept for two hundred years in a cave on Mount Celion—from the time of Roman persecution under Emperor Decius to the day when the region was ruled by Christianity—woke up, and promptly died. Their legend, told by St. Gregory the Great, concludes with the seven sleepers happily buried in the same cave.

Sts. Teresa/Thérèse. St. Teresa of Avila, St. Thérèse of Lisieux, and Blessed Teresa of Calcutta are undoubtedly three of the most important saints in the last 500 years. There is more on each of these, below.

St. Thomas. There are at least two Thomases who were profound writers in the history of Christian theology and spirituality. **St. Thomas Aquinas** (d. 1274) was a Dominican friar and theologian—the most influential theologian, in fact, in the history of the Catholic Church. Highborn in a family of knights and landowners, Thomas was drawn to join the mendicant order as a young man. His family resisted his wishes and actually imprisoned him for a year in an effort to change his mind. Thomas was known for his remarkable ability to concentrate, which aided both his scholarship and his meditation. It was said that he would often dictate to four scribes at once so that the flow of his ideas would not have to be slowed by the time it took a person to record them. His greatest work, the multivolume *Summa Theologica*, sought to blend the ideas of the Greek philosophers Aristotle and Plato with the teachings of Holy Scripture and the early church fathers. Based on these ideas, Thomas and his mentor, St. Albertus Magnus, created Scholasticism, the most dominant method in the history of theology.

Thomas à Kempis (d. 1471) led a very quiet life by comparison. A Flemish hermit, he wrote a simple book, *The Imitation of Christ*, that became the most read spiritual book of all times, next to the Bible itself. Although he experienced very little of the world for himself, Thomas's understanding of the human heart is second to none. His candidacy for beatification has unfortunately lain dormant since the seventeenth century.

St. Ursula. Her legend is one of the most tragic of the Middle Ages. This bold young Anglo-Saxon woman (lived ca. fourth century) was engaged to marry a heathen prince against her will, but she wanted nothing but a life of perpetual virginity and fidelity to Christ. She and several of her like-minded maiden friends, with thousands of other attendant virgins, sailed down the Rhine River through Cologne as pilgrims to Rome. Upon their return to Cologne, the women were violated and martyred by a band of Huns lying in wait. Later mystics claimed to see visions that corroborated this story, and in 1155 thousands of bones were discovered and claimed to be those of the young women. A church was built in their honor in Cologne, and the cult of Ursula and her companions remains strong in the Low Countries and France.

Ursula and the other maidens arrive by ship in Cologne in this painting by Hans Memling (d. 1494).

St. Valentine. This saint is just one example of how near-anonymous saints have taken on greater meaning in popular culture. We know almost nothing about Valentine, except that he was a martyr of the early church, most likely during the infamous persecutions led by the Roman emperor Decius, who ruled for only two years, from 249 to 251. There are not even reliable legends about Valentine, although he has come to inspire love in millions (at least on one day of the year!). Similarly, we know very little about St. Nicholas of Myra, named for a provincial capital in what is today the country of Turkey. The inspiration for the modern Santa Claus, Nicholas is also the patron saint of Russia and Greece. Nearly all churches—Catholic, Orthodox, and also some Protestant ones that recognize saints—celebrate the feast day of St. Nicholas on December 6. Valentine is not so fortunate; his name no longer appears on any calendars of saints.

St. Wang Cheng. The Boxer Rebellion in China (1898–1900) saw the murder of many Christians. It was an anti-Western movement that also encompassed a revolt against the missionaries. Four girls in their teens were among the martyrs. Raised in a Catholic orphanage in Wangla village, part of Hebei province, where a large wave of killings occurred, these girls were taken hostage rather than immediately killed, probably because of their youthful beauty. One of the Boxer leaders proposed marriage to Wang Cheng, who at eighteen was the eldest of the four, and she rejected him. The other girls were sixteen, fifteen, and eleven years old. After about a week of moving the young hostages around to various locations, the Boxer rebels finally returned them to their village of Wangla and demanded that they renounce Christ. They refused, saying, "We are daughters of God. We will not betray him," and were murdered. Blessed Pope John Paul II canonized all 120 martyrs of China (87 Chinese and 33 missionaries, mostly Franciscan), including St. Wang Cheng, on October 1, 2000.

Sts. Xystus. Many popes are saints, but not all. When elected, each pope takes a new name, and it has been common for popes to take the name of a previous pope, recognizing him as a spiritual forefather. **St. Xystus I** (d. ca. 127), whose name is anglicized to Sixtus I, one of the first popes, led the early church during the persecutions of the Roman emperor Trajan. **St. Xystus II** (d. 258) was pope for only a year and was also martyred, beheaded, and buried in the Roman catacombs. He is often pictured in religious art with St. Lawrence, his contemporary. Before he was martyred, Xystus II met with Lawrence, an archdeacon, and turned over the wealth of the papacy to him so that Lawrence might distribute the treasures to the poor and the needy. Four days later Lawrence was summoned and told to bring with him the treasures of the church. Dozens of previously hidden congregants joined Lawrence that day, symbolizing the true meaning of the church, but they were turned away in anger, and Lawrence was killed. **St. Xystus III** (d. 440) was a friend and correspondent of St. Augustine of Hippo, with whom he battled against many heretic groups of the day.

St. Ywi. An Irish monk of the mid-seventh century, Ywi lived in self-imposed exile for Christ, according to the model established by St. Cuthbert, the great monk of Lindisfarne, who was his teacher. Ywi, whose name is also sometimes rendered Iwi, wandered the seas with no set course or destination, expecting to spread the Good News wherever he might land and with whomever he might meet.

St. Zeno. Not to be confused with the ancient philosopher known by the same name, Zeno (d. 371) was born in Africa. He fished to feed himself while he was a hermit living along the river near Verona, Italy. Zeno fought against heresies in the church and encouraged young people to commit themselves to serving God through various ministries. He was a pastor, the first bishop of Verona, and a hard worker. But we also know that Zeno loved a good belly laugh; he was perhaps the first of the saints to show real outward joy, through laughter, as a part of his spiritual practice.

ONE RECENT ORTHODOX SAINT

This book focuses almost entirely on the saints of the Roman Catholic Church. In many instances, Catholic saints are also shared by the churches of Eastern Orthodoxy, particularly when it comes to those who lived prior to the Great Schism of 1054. Still, there are many other notable figures honored in the Orthodox churches who are worthy of mention. In the Eastern tradition, women and men are usually referred to as "glorified" rather than "canonized," but the idea and intention is the same. Here is just one of them:

St. Mother Maria Skobtsova is a Russian Orthodox saint who was glorified by act of the Holy Synod of the Ecumenical Patriarchate on January 16, 2004. Born Elizaveta Pilenko in Latvia in 1891, she became Mother Maria after what would be a lifetime of remarkable experiences for most people. Almost executed during the 1917 Russian Revolution, Elizaveta was a leader in local government, a twice-married mother of three children, and a political refugee who fled the turbulent Russian Empire for France in 1919. After her second daughter died of illness, Elizaveta, one of those amazing people who could turn unspeakable tragedy into an opportunity for deepening holiness, began to feel a calling to what she felt could be a more "broad and all-embracing motherhood."[3] As an exile in Paris, Elizaveta became fully committed to the plight of the poor, the dispossessed, the mentally ill, and anyone in need, including, perhaps most importantly, Jews who were forced to hide during the Nazi occupation. Mother Maria served those in need until the end, when she too was gassed in the Nazi concentration camp in Ravensbrück, Germany.

SELECTING A PATRON SAINT

After that quick tour, perhaps one of the saints stands out as meaningful for your life.

Sometimes a patron saint is the one for whom you were named. It is no accident that Catholics have biblical first names more often than do Protestants. Traditionally, Catholic parents have given their children names of saints and encouraged them to model themselves after the saint's virtuous example. This is first celebrated in the initiation sacrament of baptism. Paragraph 2156 of the *Catechism of the Catholic Church* reads:

> The sacrament of Baptism is conferred "in the name of the Father and of the Son and of the Holy Spirit" (Matthew 28:19). In Baptism, the Lord's name sanctifies man, and the Christian receives his name in the Church. This can be the name of a saint, that is, of a disciple who has lived a life of exemplary fidelity to the Lord. The patron saint provides a model of charity; we are assured of his intercession. The "baptismal

name" can also express a Christian mystery or Christian virtue. Parents, sponsors and the pastor are to see that a name is not given which is foreign to Christian sentiment.

Especially in the years before the Second Vatican Council, children were urged to choose the name of a patron saint upon confirmation, which usually takes place at about the age of thirteen.

Since ancient days, parents would encourage their children to choose names of saints, rather than those of secular heroes, such as athletes (St. John Chrysostom preached a sermon against such names in the early fifth century), other deities, or nonbelievers. Name day (from the Latin phrase *dies natalis*, or "day of birth") then became an annual celebration in the home, more important than a birthday—just as a saint's feast day is more important that his or her birthday. The confirmand selected a new name to celebrate becoming a new creature in Christ, and once taken, the saint's name was intended to become the child's identity in a deep and meaningful way. It also served to stimulate the child's curiosity in the life of the saint.

Today, when more than two-thirds of Catholic children go unconfirmed, it might seem that the spiritual practice of choosing a saint as a spiritual guide is too outdated to be meaningful. But it can still be a way of building and maintaining deep relationships that cross the divide between heaven and earth. Many years ago, I chose St. Francis of Assisi as my patron saint. I prayed words like those below, asking him to teach me and guide me in his unique path of following Christ.

You might choose to select a patron saint of your own. In your reading about saints and your explorations into their lives you may discover that one saint, or more, seems to speak, as it were, directly to your own life situation.

PRAYER TO A PATRON SAINT

After you have selected a patron saint, or asked a trusted spiritual adviser to select one for you, pray a prayer such as this:

Good St. _____, please witness to who I want to become, before God. Assist me and intercede for me as I seek to fulfill the promises of heaven in my life. You faced the same challenges that I face now. Your faithfulness will be a model for me on my journey to model Christ.

Or, this:

Pray for me, St. _____. Pray that I will have the courage, creativity, and happiness that come from living a holy life. Be with me this day and always as I live to understand and love my inheritance as a child of God.

TWO

The Making of a Saint

W E HAVE SEEN THE NATURAL EVOLUTION
of how heroes of the faith were easily set apart in
the early church as martyrs and saints. Eventually,
in the tenth century, the making of saints was nor-
malized, and the power to do it was consolidated in
Rome with the pope. Procedures and expectations
for canonization were really codified in 1634. They
remain basically the same, today, except for a few
additional rules and clarifications established by
Pope John Paul II in 1983.

The *Catechism of the Catholic Church* explains in
paragraph 828:

> By canonizing some of the faithful, i.e.,
> by solemnly proclaiming that they practiced
> heroic virtue and lived in fidelity to God's grace,
> the Church recognizes the power of the Spirit
> of holiness within her and sustains the hope
> of believers by proposing the saints to them
> as models and intercessors. "The saints have
> always been the source and origin of renewal
> in the most difficult moments in the Church's
> history." (John Paul II)

There are four major steps in the process of making a saint in the Roman Catholic Church: the opening of a formal case or "cause," research and investigations into that cause, beatification, and canonization.

Since the tenth century, there has always been a waiting period before a case can be opened, but the duration has differed from era to era. Until 1917, the customary waiting period before opening a case was fifty years after the person's death—so long that those who had known the subject would also likely be dead. The waiting period was seen as a way to lend objectivity to a process that had, in the early church, been based primarily on popular opinion.

Nevertheless, on several occasions a pope has accelerated the cause of a saint because of a personal relationship he had with the person. Perhaps most famously, St. Francis of Assisi's special counselor, Cardinal Ugolino, who was elected Pope Gregory IX just after the little poor man's death, presided over Francis's rapid canonization only two years later. Another rapid canonization that was known throughout Europe was that of St. Thomas Becket in 1173, less than three years after his martyrdom in the cathedral at Canterbury. In that case, Pope Alexander III, Becket's friend and confidant during the latter's many conflicts with King Henry II, oversaw a quick canonization to satisfy the pilgrims who had already made Canterbury a place for pilgrimage. More recently, Pope John Paul II sped along the process for Blessed Mother Teresa of Calcutta, his good friend and contemporary.

Today, the customary waiting period is five years after the death of the faithful one before the process may officially begin. It begins with the pope's receiving recommendations for possible beatifications from local dioceses. An appointed team of diocesan leaders and Vatican officials then investigates the life of the proposed candidate, reviewing recommendations for the opening of a case, in a process that resembles the preparing of legal briefs. The formal opening of a case is the first step toward sainthood. Ultimately, it is the pope who makes the decision to open a case, which means that further arguments will be heard for the cause. In recent memory, Pope Benedict XVI formally opened Blessed Pope John Paul II's case only a month after his predecessor's death—but that is unusual.

More common is a case like that of Mother Marianne Cope of Molokai (Hawaii), which was formally opened when Pope John Paul II decreed on April 19, 2004 that her heroic virtue had been confirmed. The German-born Cope (b. 1838) joined the Sisters of St. Francis as a young woman. She worked for most of her life with leprosy patients in Hawaii, and her cause for sainthood is being championed by dioceses on the Pacific Islands, where she is buried, and in Syracuse, New York, where the Sisters of St. Francis are headquartered.

Before 1983, when a cause for sainthood was officially assigned to one of the priests of the Congregation for the Causes of Saints in Rome, the canon lawyers became involved. A defense lawyer would prepare a brief that demonstrates the case for official sanctity, and a sort of prosecutor, called the promoter of the faith—or, colloquially, the devil's advocate—would prepare objections to and arguments against the case. Sometimes, the arguments of the devil's advocate would not be adequately satisfied and the case would stall somewhere in the Vatican. Even when cases did proceed they were occasionally subject to later review or revision.

But in 1983, Pope John Paul II changed this process from an essentially adversarial one to a historical and theological investigation only. Today, the second step in the process for making a saint, once a cause has been officially started, is for an appointed person to write the biography of the figure. The person's life is thoroughly researched using the most rigorous academic methods, including an examination of every extant piece of writing by him or her, in order to present the world with a credible "case." A famous, recent example of this was the *New York Times* bestseller, *Mother Teresa: Come Be My Light*, written by Father Brian Kolodiejchuk, MC, the postulator of the Cause of Beatification and Canonization of Mother Teresa of Calcutta.

After all of this research is done, the next step for Mother Marianne—or for any potential saint—is beatification. This process involves the gathering, reviewing, and authenticating of miracles attributed to the person under consideration. These miracles are usually healings that come after a devotee has prayed for the intercession of the candidate. In addition to attesting a miracle claim, at this stage Vatican authorities will hear testimonies from witnesses for the candidate, continue to examine the subject's writings for orthodoxy, and eventually discern whether or not miracles occurred as a result of the candidate's intercession after death or, sometimes, during life. In Mother Marianne's case, one miracle has already been attested, which led to her official beatification in 2005.

In this regard, the making of saints remains a somewhat democratic process even today. Just as popular devotion was able to make saints in the earliest centuries of the church, when people today begin to pray to a potential saint or otherwise show devotion or respect for his or her life and ministry on earth, this fuels the process toward beatification and canonization. These popular movements are very much like grassroots campaigns, as people advocate for their candidate and offer prayers to him or her. Popes do the same, as when John Paul II prayed to Edith Stein, also known as Teresa Benedicta of the Cross, at Auschwitz in 1979 just after his election as pope and almost twenty years before he officially canonized her. (Blessed John Paul II, in fact, canonized and beatified more men and women than all of the previous pontiffs combined. He was a great champion of making saints, venerating saints, and praying to them.) It is this sort of "campaigning" that not only summons the attention of church authorities but also makes it possible to accumulate evidence that the candidate has indeed helped in the answering of prayers.

Canonization is the fourth and final step in the process. It includes something very practical for believers: a declaration that this person is without a doubt with God in heaven. In other words, a saint is known with certainty to be available for prayer and assistance. St. Thérèse of Lisieux (d. 1897) had the quickest canonization in the modern era (although she may be surpassed by either Blessed Mother Teresa or Blessed John Paul II). Thérèse was declared a saint in 1925, only twenty-eight years after her death.

"The Little Flower," as she was called, was twenty-four years old when she died. Her sweetness and innocence reminded her contemporaries—the millions who read her autobiography soon after her death—of the Virgin Mary. But in a youthful and modern style, Thérèse eschewed mystical experiences as unnecessary for holiness and argued that righteousness is for all people, secular and religious. One recent biographer explains the impact that she had on the early twentieth century:

By 1915, nearly a million copies [of her autobiography, *The Story of a Soul*] were in print; a separate publication anthologized the hundreds of thousands of letters (arriving at a rate of five hundred a day, one thousand a day by 1925) that bore witness to miracles granted by Thérèse's intercession.[4]

The faithful have credited St. Thérèse with thousands of miracles over the last hundred years, most often healings from tuberculosis, the disease that took Thérèse's own life. Many today who pray to Thérèse to intercede for them claim to experience the smell of sweet flowers when in the real presence of the Little Flower.

When Blessed Mother Teresa was beatified in October 19, 2003, this was also a rapid process in response to popular demand. Pope John Paul II granted a special dispensation to open her case only two years after her death. Today, at least two posthumous miracles must be demonstrated and attributed to the intervention of the person in order to declare her or him a saint worthy of veneration. In Mother Teresa's case, when one miracle had been documented—the healing of a sick woman in India who had prayed to her—Teresa was cleared for beatification. Canonization is sure to follow soon, but a second miracle will need to be documented before that can officially happen.

THE TROUBLE WITH
POSTHUMOUS MIRACLES

In talking about the canonization of saints, it is important to highlight one important distinction. Some saints are canonized for their work on earth, and some are canonized for their "work" after death. Blessed Mother Teresa is a recent prime example of the first category. Mother Teresa lived such an obviously saintly life, completely for other people and for God, that if she had lived during the first centuries of Christianity she would have been venerated as a saint immediately upon her death. In the modern context of her death, the Church still rushed to canonize her, and more than 300,000 people crowded into St. Peter's Square in Vatican City to hear John Paul II announce that he was beatifying the small Albanian woman. "Brothers and sisters," John Paul said to the crowd, "even in our days God inspires new models of sainthood. Some impose themselves for their radicalness, like that offered by Mother Teresa of Calcutta."

In contrast, there are other figures who become known as saints only after their deaths. These men and women sometimes seem to owe as much of their popularity to the earnestness of believers as they do to real presences of sanctity. St. Foy (third century)—a child martyr from the Roman era—is one such saint. Her relics have drawn pilgrims to a remote monastery in Conques, France, for centuries. The reliquary that holds her bones is made of gold and studded with jewels, a masterpiece of Gothic art that is carefully protected today. Her posthumous deeds and healing powers have inspired poets. The cult of St. Foy has centered exclusively on the power of this child saint to perform miracles after her death. At times, Foy has performed these miracles "in person," as a spirit would enter into the natural world in order to help someone in need. Such occasions, as recorded in the late-medieval text *The Book of Miracles of Sainte Foy*, include the restoration of a man's eyes after they had been torn from his head, the reviving of a mule from death, the murder of a man who was slandering Foy, and the freeing of a man bound for hanging. The list goes on and on.

This practice was a medieval one. It does not happen today, probably because we now realize that plenty of saints showed themselves remarkable in life so as to make it unnecessary to focus attention on those who only seem to cast miracles like spells after their deaths.

HISTORICAL ACCURACY AND THE SAINTS

Anyone who attended Catholic school in the 1940s or 1950s will tell you that he or she used to know the calendar of saints by heart, before it was changed after the Second Vatican Council. On occasion, saints have been officially dropped from the calendar. When serious doubts are raised about the historical accuracy of the accounts of a saint's life, for instance, investigations are reopened, and it is possible that the saint will be removed from the approved list for veneration. This happened in systematic fashion in 1969 when Pope Paul VI reorganized the liturgical year and revised the calendar of saints.

Chief among the demoted saints in history is Catherine of Alexandria, whose famous legend left us with the term *Catherine wheel*, the instrument of her torture. It was said that after Catherine was finally beheaded, her body was carried to Mount Sinai by angels. However, today, experts believe that Catherine's story is most likely a legend; she probably never existed. But to this day, one of the most important monasteries in Christendom, located on Mount Sinai and a place of refuge for monks and icons throughout the iconoclastic wars and world wars that have plagued Europe, is named for her. The Holy Monastery of St. Catherine is, in fact, the oldest inhabited monastery in the world. The Greek and Russian Orthodox churches commemorate her today, but Rome dropped her from the Catholic liturgical calendar in 1969. In addition to Catherine, St. Ursula, St. Philomena, St. Nicholas, and eighty-nine others were also dropped at that time.

Sometimes the veneration of a saint is so ingrained that the faithful will continue to venerate a figure long after the Church has deemed his or her life to be the stuff of legend. This does not seem to bother anyone too much. Sometimes the relationship one has with a saint has little to do with historical verifiability and more to do with faith that the sorts of things we see in saints' lives are possible with God. This is an example of how believing in the saints and making them a part of our lives is one with our belief in God and what God can do.

THREE

The Blessed Virgin Mary

Jesus Christ is not known as He ought to be because Mary has been up to this time unknown.
—St. Louis de Montfort (d. 1716)

THE BLESSED VIRGIN MARY IS THE SAINT above all others. Christians surely pray for Mary's intercession more than they pray to all other saints combined. Devotion to her centers on her virtues as the Mother of God, the handmaiden of our faith, the Queen of Heaven, and a trusted nurturer of souls.

Mary is recognized as an intercessor to her Son, an exemplar of quiet and simple faith. She is, of course, the one who said to the Archangel Gabriel at the Annunciation, "Be it done to me according to thy word" (Luke 1:38, Douay-Rheims). St. Gregory Thaumaturgus (d. ca. 270) once rhapsodized in a homily on the Annunciation: "Today the whole circle of the earth is filled with joy, since the sojourn of the Holy Spirit has been realized to men."

Tradition has it that Mary, through her intimate relationship with the Holy Spirit—who inspires all divine knowledge—was far more than a receptacle womb. She was chosen by God and then initiated into the divine plan. Again, a quote from that homily by St. Gregory Thaumaturgus:

> You know, O Mary, things kept hidden from the patriarchs and prophets. You have learned, O virgin, things which were kept concealed until now from the angels. You have heard, O purest one, things of which even the choir of inspired men [Scripture writers] was never deemed worthy. Moses, and David, and Isaiah, and Daniel, and all the prophets, prophesied of Him, but the manner they knew not. Yet you alone, O purest virgin, are now made the recipient of things of which all these were kept in ignorance, and you do learn the origin of them. For where the Holy Spirit is, there are all things readily ordered.

Devotion to Mary (most of us refer to her in prayer as "The Blessed Virgin," "Holy Mother of God," or the "Blessed Virgin Mary" rather than "St. Mary") is intended to bring greater love for her son, as she is always pointing to him. Her pointing to Christ is figurative, in that her role in redemptive history is to show the way to him. However, representations in art throughout the centuries have also shown Mary literally pointing to the baby Jesus on her lap. In this sense, Mary also plays the role of a great prophet. In medieval art, as well as in Catholic religious festivals today throughout the world, you will see images and statues of the "Enthroned Virgin and Child." The Christ child sits on his mother's lap, not sleepily or playfully, as any child might sit on any mother's lap, but with Mary acting as throne for Christ the King. Mary's pose faces straight ahead and is known in Latin as *Sedes Sapientiae*, or "Throne of Wisdom." Mary is the throne for Christ, Wisdom, symbolizing the vital position she holds, then and now, in the life of Christ and for any believer who wants to know Christ more intimately.

For this reason, Mary is commonly regarded as the "Mother of God" (*Theotokos*). This title has its origins in the first centuries of Christianity. The early Church Council of Ephesus approved Mary as Mother of God in 431, and at the same time, it condemned a theologian by the name of Nestorius who had argued that Mary was only mother to the human nature of Christ.

Mary is the ideal, faithful disciple or follower of Christ—his first. As his mother, Mary possesses a faith that is often mixed with sorrow, as when she and St. Joseph presented Jesus in the temple, and St. Simeon and St. Anna foretold the messiahship of the boy; when she, Joseph, and Jesus were forced to flee to Egypt; when Jesus was lost in busy Jerusalem; when she accompanied Jesus on the way to his death at Calvary; when she witnessed the Crucifixion itself; when she helped as her son was taken down from the cross (a scene immortalized in the Pietàs of Michelangelo and others); and when her son was buried in the tomb. These seven events, described in the Gospels, are in fact known as the seven sorrows of Mary. She is often described, and prayed to, as "Our Lady of Sorrows."

Catholic teaching about the Virgin Mary is called Mariology. As is the case with all Church teaching, it has evolved over the centuries, and can sometimes be confusing. In 1854, for instance, the Church proclaimed the Immaculate Conception of Mary. Pope Pius IX defined this as "the doctrine which declares that the most Blessed Virgin Mary, in the first instant of her conception, by a singular grace and privilege of Almighty God, in view of the merits of Jesus Christ, the Savior of the human race, was preserved exempt from all stain of original sin, is a doctrine revealed by God, and therefore must be believed firmly and constantly by all the faithful." There are very fine distinctions at work here. This doctrine does not teach that the Virgin Mary was miraculously conceived. It is not doubted that Mary had a father and a mother (non-canonical gospels named them St. Joachim and St. Anne). In order to emphasize the uniqueness of Mary's role in salvation history, the doctrine of the Immaculate Conception of Mary explains that her soul was sanctified by God's grace from the moment she became human. Mary was born of Adam and Eve—as one would say in speaking metaphorically about the Christian doctrine of original sin—but her soul was never actually tainted by the mistakes of our first parents.

In 1950, another pope by the name of Pius—this time it was Pope Pius XII—declared the doctrine of Mary's Assumption to Heaven. This was the Church officially stating that the mother of Jesus was more than just a saint. Mary's assumption to heaven elevated her above all others, giving her a special place in heaven, where her body and soul are believed to have been assumed after physical death but before any corruption of the body was permitted to happen. Four years later, Mary was given the additional title of Queen of Heaven. Mariologists often quote from a sermon preached by sixth-century bishop Theoteknos of Palestine, in which he argued for these teachings centuries earlier: "Christ took His immaculate flesh from the immaculate flesh of Mary. And if He prepared a place in heaven for the Apostles, how much more then for His mother? If Enoch and Elijah were translated to heaven, how much more then should Mary, who like the moon in the midst of stars shines and excels among all prophets and Apostles?"

Eastern Orthodox churches assign other special celebrations for Mary, including the Solemnity of the Presentation of the Mother of God, a feast day usually observed in late November. This honor refers to a legend from the early church that the preschool-age Mary was presented at the temple in Jerusalem, just as her son later was, and she precociously learned from and taught the scholars and priests of the temple, just as her son later did.

PRAYING WITH THE BLESSED VIRGIN MARY

We can ask Mary for her help and intercession on our spiritual journeys, and in our times of trouble and decision. She is a teacher, a companion, and an intercessor who any Christian should want to have in his or her corner.

St. Paul wrote letters asking believers to pray to God on his behalf. This was an innovation of Paul that stood in contrast to the Judaism from which he grew; the community of saints, both on earth and in heaven, may speak to God and petition God on our behalf. Paul said to the people in Rome: "Join me in earnest prayer to God on my behalf" (Romans 15:30). He said to the people in Corinth: "Join in helping us by your prayers, so that many will give thanks on our behalf for the blessing granted us through the prayers of many" (2 Corinthians 1:11). To the Ephesians he wrote: "Pray in the Spirit at all times in every prayer and supplication. To that end keep alert and always persevere in supplication for all the saints" (Ephesians 6:18). And to the church at Colossae he said: "Devote yourselves to prayer, keeping alert in it with thanksgiving. At the same time pray for us as well" (Colossians 4:2–3).

In that same spirit, we can say, "Mary, pray for us."

There are hundreds of books already available on how to pray the rosary, the world's most popular prayer and the most common way that Catholics pray to Mary. Instead of recapping here what is readily available elsewhere, consider this short, additional way of addressing our concerns to Our Lady.

PRAYER TO OUR LADY OF FIFTH AVENUE

The following prayer accompanies the statue of Mary and the child Jesus that was dedicated at St. Thomas (Episcopal) Church on Fifth Avenue in New York City in 1991. The statue is approximately four feet tall. It was created by a Benedictine nun, Mother Concordia Scott, and given by the parish to mark the fifteenth anniversary of their rector.

I come to you, Holy Mother,
to ask your prayers for _____.

You give us all encouragement to approach you
as your children, whose brother, your son
Jesus Christ, we claim as our blessed Savior
and yours.

Help me now, I ask you, with a prayer
to Him on my behalf and for His sake.
Amen.

FOUR

More Ways to Pray with the Saints

CELEBRATING THEIR FEAST DAYS

Throughout the Church, special days known as feast days are set aside for remembering and honoring one or more of the saints. A feast day is usually the day recognized as the saint's birthday in heaven, or day of new life—in other words, the day he or she died on earth. A feast day is primarily a liturgical celebration, but one may also use private prayers and remembrances found in the devotional books of many traditions on these special days.

October 4 is always highlighted on my calendar, as it is the feast day of St. Francis of Assisi, my patron saint. I usually give a talk about his life and spiritual vitality in church on that day, and I love participating in the "Blessing of the Animals" that we also celebrate on that day (or on the Sunday closest to October 4).

It can be meaningful to celebrate a saint's feast day together with friends, family, or in your parish. You may want to choose a saint as patron of your family and learn about him or her. Find a popular image or icon of your saint and talk together about the symbolism in the depiction. Ask the children and perhaps even extended family members to participate by each researching some aspect of the person's life. On the actual day, create a home celebration.

The following dates represent selected annual celebrations in both the Western and Eastern churches for some of the saints discussed in detail throughout this book. When the name for the feast differs in the churches, the Eastern name is given in parentheses, but in all cases, the date given for the feast is according to the Roman calendar (of the West).

January 2	Basil the Great and Gregory Nazianzen
January 17	Antony of Egypt
January 24	Francis de Sales
January 28	Thomas Aquinas
February 23	Polycarp
March 3	Katharine Drexel (on U.S. calendar only)
March 17	Patrick
March 25	The Annunciation
April 4	Isidore of Seville
April 29	Catherine of Siena
May 25	Venerable Bede
June 29	Peter and Paul (jointly)
July 11	Benedict of Nursia
July 22	Mary Magdalene

July 23	Bridget of Sweden
July 31	Ignatius of Loyola
August 11	Clare of Assisi
August 15	The Assumption of Mary (The Dormition of Our Lady)
August 20	Bernard of Clairvaux
August 28	Augustine of Hippo
August 29	John the Baptist
September 8	Birth of Mary
September 29	Michael, Gabriel, and Raphael (jointly)
September 30	Jerome
October 1	Thérèse of Lisieux
October 4	Francis of Assisi
October 15	Teresa of Avila
November 1	All Saints' Day
November 13	Frances Xavier Cabrini (on U.S. calendar only)
November 16	Margaret of Scotland
November 17	Elizabeth of Hungary
December 13	Lucia
December 14	John of the Cross
December 28	The Holy Innocents
December 29	Thomas Becket

TWO PRAYERS FOR USE ON ANY FEAST DAY

The following prayers are slight variations on prayers in common use throughout Catholic churches on the feast days of saints.

O God, who has brought us near to an innumerable company of angels and to the spirits of just men and women made perfect: Grant us during our earthly pilgrimage to abide in their fellowship, and in our heavenly country to become partakers of their joy; through Jesus Christ our Lord, who liveth and reigneth with thee and the Holy Spirit, one God, now and for ever. *Amen.*

O Almighty God, who by thy Holy Spirit has made us one with thy saints in heaven and on earth: Grant that in our earthly pilgrimage we may ever be supported by this fellowship of love and prayer, and may know ourselves to be surrounded by their witness to thy power and mercy.

We ask this for the sake of Jesus Christ, in whom all our intercessions are acceptable through the Spirit, and who liveth and reigneth for ever and ever. *Amen.*

LIGHTING VIGIL CANDLES

Candle lighting, another ancient practice, is a way of prayer. Long after our attention has moved on to other things, a lit votive candle symbolizes the intention of our love for God in Christ and the presence of our request before heaven. *Votive* comes from the Latin word *votum*, meaning vow, but *vigil*—a much better word for this practice—means watchfulness.

Votive or vigil candles are usually considered symbols of Christ, the Light in the darkness, but they also can be powerful symbols of our own desire to be imitators of Christ, the true Light. When used in prayer, a candle can also show our persistence and continual desire to be with God, to listen for God's will, and to seek the intercession of one of the saints. Many Christians from all denominations have small spaces called home altars where vigil candles are often kept and used for prayer. Like the psalmist, we may say, "Let my prayer be counted as incense before you, and the lifting up of my hands as an evening sacrifice" (Psalm 141:2).

February 2 is known as Candlemas on the Roman Catholic calendar. This feast celebrates the presentation of Jesus in the temple in Jerusalem. On Candlemas, candles traditionally receive a special blessing as we remember St. Simeon's prophetic words upon seeing the child Jesus, whom he called "a light for revelation to the Gentiles and for glory to your people Israel" (Luke 2:32). Before you get started, you should offer a blessing over your candles, sanctifying them for this purpose.

God of light, light to the nations,
light that reaches into all darkness,
use these candles to illuminate us.
May the light of our prayers always be with
　You,
quietly in Your holy presence,
and may we always be
reflected in Your true Light.
Amen.

CONCLUSION

Be imitators of me, as I am of Christ.
—St. Paul, 1 Corinthians 11.1

IN *CHRIST RECRUCIFIED*, the twentieth-century
Greek novelist Nikos Kazantzakis portrays a small
village enacting a Passion play. The local Orthodox
priest and other village notables assign the various
parts in the play to people in the village who seem
to fit the characters (St. Peter, St. John, Christ, the
Virgin Mary, Judas Iscariot, and so on), both in
physical appearance and in spirit or temperament.

Each person has one year to prepare for his
or her part in the play, and the play itself is of
the utmost importance to the members of this iso-
lated, insular village. In the following passage, the
priest instructs the local proprietor of a café as to
his role:

> You, Kostandis, are the man we have chosen
> to be James, the austere disciple of Christ. A
> heavy burden, a divine burden; bear it with dig-
> nity, do you hear? Do not dishonor the Apostle.
> From today you must become a new man,
> Kostandis. You are good, but you must become

better. More honest, more affable. Come to church more often. Put less barley in the coffee. Stop cutting the slabs of Turkish delight in two and selling the halves as wholes. Above all, take care not to beat your wife, because from today you are not only Kostandis, but also, and above all, James the Apostle. You understand? Do you?[5]

This is how the saints are supposed to inspire us. We are supposed to model our lives after their examples in very real ways. In fact, the lives of the saints have always inspired readers of books to greater godliness, even through imitation. It is my hope that this short book, and its stories of saints, has so inspired you.

There are many other good books about the saints—and, of course, many of the saints wrote books of their own that make for important spiritual reading. For example, St. Francis de Sales once quipped that the *Spiritual Exercises* of St. Ignatius of Loyola had probably made as many saints (those who followed its precepts) as the book had letters. And St. Francis de Sales's own book *Introduction to the Devout Life* is also a handbook for sainthood. It details how to approach God through the life of the Church and through prayer, how to avoid and overcome common temptations to sin, and the sixteen most important virtues. It has inspired millions over the centuries.

The Little Flowers of Saint Francis of Assisi has inspired me the most of all the books of stories of saints. It presents the early Franciscan movement, including St. Francis, St. Clare, St. Giles of Assisi, and many others, as they modeled their lives after Jesus.

In other words, there are many, many books to read. Thank you for joining me in this one. Now, you may want to go and find others. Most important of all, I hope that you will allow the stories of the saints to impact your life.

And don't forget to speak to them—these champions of our faith who are in heaven cheering us on the path to God. The communion of saints is all around us, all the time. They are listening, available, right before us.

NOTES

1. Richard P. McBrien, *Lives of the Saints: From Mary and St. Francis of Assisi to John XXIII and Mother Teresa* (New York: HarperCollins, 2003), 384.

2. McBrien, 123.

3. Quoted by Jim Forest in the introduction to *Mother Maria Skobtsova: Essential Writings*, trans. Richard Pevear and Larissa Volokhonsky (Maryknoll, NY: Orbis Books, 2003), 20.

4. Kathryn Harrison, *Saint Therese of Lisieux* (New York: Viking Press, 2003), 3.

5. Nikos Kazantzakis, *Christ Recrucified*, trans. Jonathan Griffin (London, England: Faber & Faber, 1962), 22. This novel is titled *The Greek Passion* in U.S. editions.

Assumption: Catholic doctrine formally adopted by Pope Pius XII in 1950 stating that the Virgin Mary did not experience death but was "assumed" into heaven. The Feast of the Assumption of Mary is celebrated on August 15.

Beatification: A formal declaration from the Holy See that a deceased person should be *venerated* for the righteous life he or she led. This is a necessary step prior to *canonization*, although not all those who are beatified are canonized.

Blessed: Appropriate title for one who has been *beatified.*

Canonization: A formal declaration from the Holy See that a *blessed*, deceased person is a saint and that veneration of him or her is efficacious for all Christians.

Congregation for the Causes of Saints: Located in Rome, this ecclesiastical body is convened after a person's *beatification* in order to investigate the cause for sainthood.

Cults of the saints: Popular movements of support for the veneration of a saint.

Doctor of the Church: Saint who is also given this additional title by the pope or the church in recognition of the person's special gifts for teaching the faith. St. Teresa of Avila was the first woman declared a Doctor of the Church, while St. Thérèse of Lisieux is the most recent.

Feast day: A day set aside each year for liturgically honoring a saint. A saint's feast day is usually the day of his or her death, which is also the day of his or her new, or eternal, life.

Mariology: Study and teaching of the doctrines on the subject of the Blessed Virgin Mary. Marian is the adjective used to describe the qualities, features, and influences of the Virgin.

Novena: Special petitionary prayer repeated on nine successive days, modeled after the prayer of the disciples of Jesus who waited in the upper room for nine days after Christ's resurrection.

Patron saint: A saint who offers a special relationship to people of a particular city, region, country, church, occupation, or physical/spiritual need. This term is also used for a saint who is chosen or given to an individual at baptism.

Second Vatican Council: The most important ecumenical (meaning that it encompassed all rites, or expressions, of the Catholic Church) council since late antiquity. Convened by Pope John XXIII in 1962, Vatican II called for dramatic liturgical reforms, new roles for the laity in worship and religious life, greater outreach to the poor, and ecumenical openness to people of other Christian branches and other faiths.

Stigmata: From a Latin word meaning "marks," signifies the five wounds of Jesus from the torture of the crucifixion: one in each hand, one in each foot, and a pierce in the side. The same wounds have appeared inexplicably on the bodies of saints, sometimes accompanied by bleeding. St. Francis of Assisi was the first stigmatic.

Theotokos: Greek word and name for the Blessed Virgin Mary: "Mother of God."

Veneration: Catholic doctrine makes a clear distinction between veneration, which is due to saints, and worship, which is due only to God. To venerate literally means "to honor."

Vigil lights (candles): For millennia, burning candles have represented prayer and devotion. The burning flame represents the fervor of the devoted and continues the "vigil" of prayer long after the devoted has gone from that place. The lighting of candles is popular form of devotion throughout the world; the candles are usually placed before images of saints or shrines or within side chapels set aside for devotion to a saint or saints.

ABOUT PARACLETE PRESS

WHO WE ARE

Paraclete Press is a publisher of books, recordings, and DVDs on Christian spirituality. Our publishing represents a full expression of Christian belief and practice—from Catholic to Evangelical, from Protestant to Orthodox.

We are the publishing arm of the Community of Jesus, an ecumenical monastic community in the Benedictine tradition. As such, we are uniquely positioned in the marketplace without connection to a large corporation and with informal relationships to many branches and denominations of faith.

WHAT WE ARE DOING

Books Paraclete publishes books that show the richness and depth of what it means to be Christian. Although Benedictine spirituality is at the heart of all that we do, we publish books that reflect the Christian experience across many cultures, time periods, and houses of worship. We publish books that nourish the vibrant life of the church and its people—books about spiritual practice, formation, history, ideas, and customs.

We have several different series, including the best-selling Paraclete Essentials and Paraclete Giants series of classic texts in contemporary English; A Voice from the Monastery—men and women monastics writing about living a spiritual life today; award-winning poetry; best-selling gift books for children on the occasions of baptism and first communion; and the Active Prayer Series that brings creativity and liveliness to any life of prayer.

Recordings From Gregorian chant to contemporary American choral works, our music recordings celebrate sacred choral music through the centuries. Paraclete distributes the recordings of the internationally acclaimed choir Gloriæ Dei Cantores, praised for their "rapt and fathomless spiritual intensity" by *American Record Guide*, and the Gloriæ Dei Cantores Schola, which specializes in the study and performance of Gregorian chant. Paraclete is also the exclusive North American distributor of the recordings of the Monastic Choir of St. Peter's Abbey in Solesmes, France, long considered to be a leading authority on Gregorian chant.

Videos Our videos offer spiritual help, healing, and biblical guidance for life issues: grief and loss, marriage, forgiveness, anger management, facing death, and spiritual formation.

Learn more about us at our website: www.paracletepress.com, or call us toll-free at 1-800-451-5006.

 SCAN TO READ MORE

ALSO AVAILABLE IN THIS SERIES

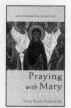

PRAYING WITH MARY
Mary Ford-Grabowsky

80 pages   ISBN: 978-1-61261-137-2
$24.95 (pack of 5), Small paperback

PRAYING THE HOLY SCRIPTURES
M. Basil Pennington OCSO

64 pages   ISBN: 978-1-61261-141-9
$24.95 (pack of 5), Small paperback

PRAYING WITH ICONS
Linette Martin

64 pages   ISBN: 978-1-61261-058-0
$24.95 (pack of 5), Small paperback

PRAYING THE JESUS PRAYER
Frederica Mathewes-Green

64 pages   ISBN: 978-1-61261-059-7
$24.95 (pack of 5), Small paperback

Available from most booksellers or through
Paraclete Press: www.paracletepress.com
1-800-451-5006.